OPTIONS TRADING START UP GUIDE

Learn How to Start Making Money and Profit with Options Trading-Binary Options-Stock Options-Index Options-Future Options-ETF Options-Currency Options

by

CONOR MATHEWS

TABLE OF CONTENTS

INTRODUCTION

Binary options is a form of trading in which prices of currencies, commodities, futures, stocks, and indices are traded. Still, binary options trading is not to be confused with Forex and stocks trading, since there are certain differences between the markets. Binary options are an easier form, in the sense that they are easier to understand, but as with every market, they require a serious approach as well. What characterizes binary options is that traders do not buy the assets; they simply invest or "bet" on whether an asset will rise or drop in value. They place trades on the potential price increase or decrease, but never really own the asset.

Therefore, binary options is often compared to gambling, and it took a long time for the market to establish itself as a trading market, defending itself by proving that it is far removed from a game of chance. The truth is that it is a little bit of both, and it depends on how traders see it. If traders participate in the market as individuals with a trading plan and a clear strategy, it certainly classifies as trading. Nevertheless, if traders approach the market like a game and make random trades, they classify as gamblers.

There is no clear-cut line in the options market since it is flexible and depends solely on how the trader approaches it. Still, binary options is one of the most popular markets, right next to the trillion dollar Forex industry, and they appeal to many market participants, especially to beginners who find it easier to understand than the stock or Forex market for example.

Numerous assets are at the disposal of traders, and they can switch from one to the other in no time. The biggest advantage of binary options is that they consist of Yes and No questions. Traders simply have to decide if the price of a certain asset is going up with *yes*, or down with *no*. These yes and no questions are called call and put options.

Binary options can be traded from anywhere in the world, at any time. Simply make an account, make a small deposit, and you are ready to go. This guide on binary options gives you step-by-step insight into the market, from account choice to complicated trading strategies.

In the eyes of the public, binary options is seen as a money-making machine, but that is not always the case. A trader needs to spend some time in the market and know the market to make a lucrative side income with trading. There are plenty of things to learn about the market and the most crucial things to know are discussed below in this mini-edition.

If you are really serious about becoming a binary options trader, then this start-up guide can help you in developing a real trading career. This guide is aimed at all those who want to succeed in the market and who are ready to commit to the cause. This guide can open the doors to the market and its secrets, if you are willing to learn, study, and engage in market activities.

This guide is an eye-opener for all those who think that binary options can be traded randomly and that luck is the only factor. The truth looks a little bit different, and the market requires a strategic approach and informed traders in order to produce high profits. Read our guide in order to familiarize yourself with the binary options world and what advantages and disadvantages are waiting for you. Learn how to become a true professional and expert in a market that is full of profitable opportunities.

CHAPTER 1: WHAT IS BINARY OPTIONS

The binary options market evolved as a form of trading in the financial market in the last fifteen years and represents one of the biggest markets in existence, next to the unbeatable Forex market.

The binary options market is in many ways similar to Forex, but the main difference is that you do not buy stocks, goods, commodities, currencies, or indices. You simply place a bet how an asset will perform in the market. You do not actually buy or sell the assets, since they are never really yours, but you participate by investing your predictions. For example, when you place a trade on the USDEUR, you never really own the USD, but you bet on the possibility that it will rise or drop in value.

The binary options market is a controversial one since, in many countries, it is regarded as gambling and bookmaking. Still, some disagree and call it true trading. There is a little bit of truth in both of these theories, since making predictions makes it a form of gambling, but the strategies and mathematical calculations involved make it a form of trading. Even if not completely redeemed from the gambling market label, options trading has come a long way in defending its status as a sincere trading market. The results are visible all over the world since more governments and people now accept it as trading.

Just like the Forex market, the binary options market also has an extremely high entertainment factor since it drives up the adrenaline of market participants, and the uncertainty and risk contribute to the fun. The fact that significant profits can come out of this makes is even better. People enter the business for different reasons; some of them are there for the potential money, others for fun, and onesome simply out of curiosity.

Thanks to the Internet revolution, binary options, along Forex, became widespread, and everyone who has an Internet connection and is willing can participate. The market grew out of proportion and now has millions of participants who hope to be the ones who will make a small fortune out of their trades.

The market is a well-oiled machine, lacking neither supply nor demand since it is overloaded with service providers and service users, just like Forex. Many Forex brokers offer binary options services along with Forex, and you can do both from one platform and with one broker. The Forex and binary options platforms are compatible, and one can be used for both types of trading.

Binary options are a simple form of trading in general, and that is why many people are drawn to it. It does not diversify as the Forex market does, but once you dig deeper, you will discover that the market rests on complex structures and theories which can be very helpful in trading. So, traders who want to make real money in the industry have to hit the books to catch up on the different strategies and analyses that can be applied in the market.

As a beginner, you should familiarize yourself with the basics of binary options in order to get a grip on how things work. This guide can help you to develop basic options trading skills.

CHAPTER 2: THE BASICS OF BINARY OPTIONS

As we said, options traders neither buy nor sell assets, but they decide whether a price will rise or drop. Binary options seem easy to grasp since it is limited to several moves, but the truth behind these moves can be somewhat tricky. The several options types require explanation and, as a beginner, you should know to differentiate between the different options which can be traded.

Sometimes traders are forced to trade without complete information, but it is still better to have an overview of what might happen based on previous experiences or background knowledge. Before placing a trade, traders should familiarize themselves with how many tradable assets are at their disposal. Traders usually opt for indices, commodities, individual stocks, currencies, and commodities. When it comes to indices, the most traded are NASDAQ, FTSE 100, and DAX. Major currencies also rank high.

Gold and silver and copper are the forerunners when considering commodities. Traders can opt for fixed commodity prices, which is recommended for beginners, until they learn how to operate in a fluctuating market.

The market especially fluctuates when trading individual stocks or shares. This shaky ground can scare a beginner easily since the prices move up and down all day. Of course, when it comes to trading stocks, the most popular are stocks high-profile companies like Google, Facebook, Apple, Microsoft, etc. The big fish from the banking sector are not excluded, since the highly volatile bank stocks like Barclay Banks and J P Morgan are also at the top of the list. Having learned what assets are available, let us discover what types of trading are at our disposal.

The High/Low

This is the type of trading that is especially appealing to beginners since it only refers to a simple yes or no answer. They are called call and put options as well. You either bet that a price will go up or down for the asset you chose, within the timeframe you selected. In options trading, it is especially common to trade short-term trades that only last 30 seconds. High/Low options are usually traded on 5-minute to 15-minute timeframes, but could trade over a whole day. If your prediction is correct by the time the trade expires, you win, and if not, you lose.

For example, you opt for a commodity asset, place a trade that the commodity price will rise, and set a 15-minute expiry period. If the asset price increases within the 15 minutes, you will gain a share of profit. The same applies to the opposite situation where you believe that the commodity price will drop in value. In that case, you simply buy a put option and wait for the outcome.

The different timeframes for this option vary, and they can be 30 and 60 seconds, 5 and 15 minutes, 1 or 2 hours, a whole day, a week, a month, and, sometimes, a year. In practice, however, no one actually trades with a year-long expiry period.

The rule is to make educated guesses, which means that you should have some knowledge of how the price is supposed to move. You can extract this information from economic news releases, or by analyzing the market's past behavior. Gathering information is the first step before you engage on a trading adventure.

This type of trading can bring in up to 80% returns since binaries are known for high return rates. The higher the pay-out rate, the higher the risk, so do not get easily carried away when you see a 90% and above return rate.

The one/No Touch

The price is usually within a marked range and moves around. With a touch option, you forecast whether the price will touch the limit on either side during the timeframe of your choice.

This type of trading is riskier than the High/Low options type since it requires more precision. Also, with this option, you can opt for the price range that will break the lower range lever or the upper price level.

The pay-out rate is extremely high, which indicates the level of risk with trading in this way. The pay-out can be as high as 300% or 500%, but that is solely determined by the broker. The broker company assesses how risky the trades are and what percentage they are willing to pay.

One more thing, when the price touches the range you predicted and invested in before expiration, you can immediately relax since you won. You do not have to wait until the end since your goal is already achieved. It is only important that the price touches the specified amount, or range, for at least one second. What happens afterward does not affect you; even if the price crawls back to the initial position, you still win.

Back in the day, brokers used to set the target prices for selections from which you could choose, but since recently, brokers have enabled traders to specify the target price themselves. This move was better for the entire industry since it resulted in a more transparent market, preventing brokers from suggesting impossible target prices.

Range or Channel Trading

This kind of trading gives you pre-defined ranges for price movements. You can select a given range, and if the price is in the range of your choice when the trade expires, you win. As opposed to touch options, the prices for ranges are solely defined by the broker.

The different ranges are divided by color, so that they will appear in different colors on the chart. These kinds of trades are somewhat longer since the brokers also determines expiry periods, and, most of the time, they are set from half an hour to 24 hours.

As with the touch option, which has the counterpart no-touch option, the range trades also come in pairs, and the counterpart is out-of-range trading. When you opt for this variety, you simply bet that the price will not reach the pre-defined range.

You should bear in mind, that, as a beginner, you should try the call and put options first, and, only when you gained substantial experience, should you trade no-touch and range trading.

Range trading is not that common, and you will find that not ever broker offers it.

Expiry Periods

We have already indicated the expiry periods and timeframes possible with binary options, but let's take a closer look at them. One-minute periods are very often selected by traders, especially when trading put/call options. The charm of this trading timeframe is that you can make money in one minute, but one should not forget that it can also be lost in the same amount of time.

This timeframe is especially convenient for informed trading, when you know how the market is going to react. It requires quick judgment and quick action, which makes it highly entertaining. Beginners and those who do not understand strategy should avoid this expiry period, since they will need more time to figure out the market movement. It is designed for trading small price movements, and traders usually place multiple trades at once, following strong trends in order to make a visible profit, not just peanuts, from one trade.

The recently added 30-second trading refers to turbo trading, where the same rules apply as for 1-minute trading, but in shorter form. If you are the kind of trader who cannot wait for long for the results, then this is your game.

Long-term trades in binary options refer to day-long, hour-long, week-long, and month-long trading. Even if there is a year expiration period, it rarely happens in the options industry.

As a beginner, it advisable to start with this kind of trading, holding positions for a day or week, since these trades are steadier and do not fluctuate as intensely.

Many beginners start out with short-term trades to see how well they handle it, but the truth is, it is risky to start with the shortest expiry periods since you could lose all of your investment in a series of short-term trades.

The ladder pattern is yet another recent invention in the industry, which refers to price levels given at equal distances from each other. Since it looks like that they create a ladder, it is conveniently called the ladder. For this trading type, you are required to choose three different target prices, with three different expiry periods. Every target price has its own return rate guarantee. Of course, as it always is in the industry, the return rate is higher if the risk is higher.

When engaging in ladder trading, the broker lets the client, or the trader, pick the strike price and the expiry period, whereby they determine the return percentage policy. Pair trading is also part of the binary world, and it involves placing trades on the potential performance of a stock or currency. Your job is to decide which asset is going to perform better, so you might bet that Google will be better than Facebook.

CHAPTER 3: PROFESSIONAL BROKERS ONLY

As a beginner, you have to do a lot of background checks if you want to be in the options industry. The right broker is going to be your backbone, so you have to find a good one in order to make it in the highly-decentralized market.

The Forex and options markets are fertile grounds for many manipulators and fictitious brokers--scammers who have no intention to treat you as a trader, but rather as their source of income. There are so many broker companies that have been closed down for various reasons. Some went bankrupt, and others cheated traders and clients with Ponzi scheme-behavior.

Nevertheless, many brokers out there are doing a good job, because brokerage is really their job, not just a cover-up for fraud. Those are the brokers you should be looking for. There are several characteristics that define a good broker.

The first thing to do is to check if the binary options broker has a license and find out who their supervisor is. This also means that you should check on the quality of the supervisor and license issuer. Regulatory agencies usually make sure that brokers behave according to the law, and that they keep your money separate from their own. Their goal is to maintain a safe and transparent market, and they also issue warnings to the public when they discover that a broker has engaged in malpractice. Other people, like friends and family, who are in the business can give you valuable information on which broker has a good reputation.

It is important to know that you are only protected by the laws of your country, which means that if you sign up with an international broker, you need to see if they obtained a local license for their operations. You can check your broker's history to see if they have any records of illegal behavior (have they been ever suspended, fined, etc.).

The most important thing is that the broker behaves according to the law and does an honest job. Now, let's see what other qualities a broker should have which will benefit you as a trader.

The first thing is the trading platform. It is the most important tool, and you should feel comfortable with using the platform. Some prefer the most popular MT4 platform since it comes with all necessary options and is, indeed, universal, while others prefer customized, more intuitive platforms designed by the broker.

Whatever the case, just look for a platform that you like the most, as long as it is compatible with all the tools and options necessary for optimal trading results. The trading platform should also come with the corresponding mobile trading app, which should not be a problem since almost all brokers offer it. Mobile trading accounts for 50% of overall trading, given that many people like to trade on the go. It is very convenient and enables you to take a look at your trades wherever you are.

As soon as you enter the business, you will notice that there are different types of accounts. If you are a beginner, you should stick to the Starters package and the account that is relevant to your trading experience. With time, you can switch to an upgraded account which will offer you more possibilities.

As a binary options trader, you will also need to have a variety of choices, which means that you want a broker who offers numerous assets. For example, some brokers are so good that they have 200+ assets on their list. Different commodities, currencies, indices and stocks should be offered to you, in order to have a fair chance in the market.

We also mentioned that the binary options market, or the brokers, offer fixed return rates. This can be an advantage since you can know in advance what to expect. Choose a broker who offers a high return rate, but be careful not to pick a broker who offers over 90 % return rate. A 90% return rate is not quite possible, and you should know that such a broker will never be able to keep their word. They will either try to scam you, or display trades that are impossible to win.

As a beginner, you will need appropriate assistance until you fit in with the whole market, so good customer service is key. Customer support systems are usually available around the clock, and you should be able to call them anytime you encounter a problem with the platform, account, or money transfer. Some customer support systems left the clients waiting for too long, and that is unacceptable in this rapid market, where you depend on time. Therefore, you might test different customer support systems of different brokers by contacting them before you sign up, to see how they handle your case.

A good broker will always keep their clients' funds separate from the company's finances to avoid the risk of mingling the different assets. This assures you that your funds will be kept safe, and that they will not "get lost somehow."

What traders especially appreciate is a fast pay-out. Once you make a profit, you want to be sure that you will get your money on time. There are brokers who handle withdrawal requests very fast, even in 24 hours. They make no excuses and pay you on time. Bad brokers come up with reasons for why they cannot pay you, and they make it sound like it is your fault. Read customer reviews to see how brokers handle their withdrawal requests.

Bonuses are what attracts customers the most. They account for a large number of clients and are the best marketing tool of a broker. The thing is, a good bonus policy can upgrade a broker's reputation tremendously. But this medal also has two sides. Namely, some brokers use bonuses to lure customers, and, when it comes to pay-outs, they do not pay. Many traders apply for a bonus without reading the terms and conditions, and that is a huge mistake. The T&C can sometimes be tricky, and a lot of requirements have to be met in order to get the bonus money, so it is recommended to carefully read and study a broker's bonus policy before applying for one. Good brokers will always have clearly defined bonus terms, stick to them, and pay you out accordingly.

Another thing you might want to take a look at when choosing your broker is their banking options. The majority of brokers offer numerous payment methods, from wire transfer to several e-wallets. And, again, take a double look at their deposit and withdraw policy, because some of the brokers require high fees for money transfers, while others do it for free. Look for brokers who have a minimum or no transfer fees because with time it will save you a lot of money. The binary options industry is tough, and you need a good, professional broker as a safety net and guide.

CHAPTER 4: BINARY OPTIONS BEGINNER GUIDELINES AND THE DEMO ACCOUNT

There is no rule that prohibits you from signing up with more than one broker. This can actually be a good idea in order to compare the services of different brokers, and you will have access to more assets with different price quotes possibly.

When you start examining different brokers, you will notice that the minimum deposits vary. You will encounter brokers who let you in with as little as $10, those who require around $100, and some even more than $1000.

The majority of brokers have three standard accounts, the beginner account, starter account, and a VIP account. The higher the account type, the bigger the price, but you get to enjoy different perks and extra tools, which are not available for example with the starters account.

Beginners are advised to start with small investments, and it does not make sense to get an advanced account immediately, until you learn all the account features. Since we reduced the circle to brokers who are legitimate and decent business partners, we advise you to choose several to increase your success rate in general. Also, you can compare their offers to see the differences. The average minimum deposit is $100 (but can be higher or lower).

The Demo Account

The demo account has become a standard part of the options and Forex industry, and all brokers offer it as an assisting tool to help beginners master the different options which await them on a real trading platform. The demo account is a simulated version of real-time market events and is aimed for traders who have zero trading experience. It is free, and any interested party can join. The demo account might not portray things exactly as they are on the market, and many traders reported back that it was very different than the real market, but it provides a basis to explore the platform. That is the main goal of a demo account. There you can learn how to place trades and how to buy and to sell options with no risk of losing real money. You trade with virtual money on the demo account. It is the perfect opportunity to develop trading skills, like how to open the trading platform.

CHAPTER 5: WHAT OPTIONS ARE FOUND ON THE PLATFORM?

Many trading platforms offer a nice set of options for you, which facilitate the trading process. These options are very important, and they have to be used, since the manual handling of trades will not always cover it. It is mandatory to familiarize yourself with the options and tools at your disposal.

The Stop Loss and Take Profit method is the easiest one and has saved many traders from unnecessary losses. This option is easy to find and enables you to leave the computer or laptop while the trade is still on. When you place a trade, you can simply activate the Stop Loss option, whereby you enter the amount at which you would like to stop the loss if the trade turns against your favor. In that way, the computer will automatically close the trade, once it hits the price you entered previously. This means that your trade will not cost you more than planned. The same goes for the Take Profit option, whereby you enter the amount of money you would like to take if the trade reaches the desired price.

Trading signals are some of the most useful options. You can subscribe to get e-mail alerts or SMS alerts every time the market is significantly moving. Trading signals inform you on the state of play and the right time to place a couple of trades. Bollinger Bands are one of the top trading signals in binary options. These signals let you know when you are dealing with an overbought or oversold market. Bollinger Bands are based on a three-line set-up. One line shows average action in the trending market, and the other two indicate when the trend is deviating from normal, and they are called band lines.

When you gain some experience with Bollinger Bands and become an advanced trader, you can also use oscillators, which are more precise, like the RSI oscillator. Still, while at the beginner stage, it is better to stick to simple trend signals, because a lot of market knowledge is required to use more complex options.

Trading signals are often used with binary options trading, and you have to be careful with that too. Never make a deposit for a robot which does not show all the settings. Also, do not believe the testimonials and comments below the ad, because most of the time, they are fictitious.

Automated trading is tricky, because a third party is in charge of your account, which means you allow software to place trades without your consent. If using automated assistance, make sure you have a high-quality tool or software, even if you have to pay for it more.

There are also different apps that let you know what is going on in the market. They observe the market for you, and let you know about the events taking place. But not all apps are good.

You want to look for a very good app, which will collect useful data on your behalf and buy and sell positions automatically for you. The trick is to find a high-performing app which will make the right decisions. It is a form of automated trading and needs to be carefully selected.

You need to slowly introduce automated trading, if you want to do it right. The biggest secret is to know how these automated tools work. If you do not understand it, do not use it. Many traders get carried away by the different ads that travel the Internet stating that automated tools can do the job for you, but the truth is, they sometimes fail. Moreover, low-quality tools will always fail and make you lose your investments.

CHAPTER 6: BINARY OPTIONS ROBOTS

The most revolutionary tool for automated trading is the invention of Expert Advisors, or robots which can come with the platform, or be bought and installed separately. Options robots are supposed to trade for you, based on their data processing. They are developed by experienced traders and experts using an algorithmic system which is supposed to predict prices based on their data processing skills and calculations. This sounds just too good to be true, and, in most cases, it is. Robots have to be extremely good to be able to predict the market.

Unfortunately, many pretend to offer robot tools, but they design the robots to fail you. Some robots, especially those developed by crooked brokers, will work against your favor and make you lose on purpose, which means profit for the broker.

Another problem with robots (even those built with honest intentions) is the fact that they are often not able to predict the market and that many technical obstacles hinder their performance. For example, a robot, if it does not run smoothly, can freeze during a trade and not react how it was supposed to, losing you potential profits.

Also, robots that perform well, have a good reputation, and get excellent customer feedback have to be handled with care. Therefore, robot assistance is only recommended for experienced traders. It is highly unlikely that you, as a beginner, can operate the robot properly. It takes more than just activate it. You still have to know the market. The most ideal thing is to combine manual trading with an options robot and never let it trade completely on its own. You have to observe the behavior of the automated software, and when it starts behaving oddly, you can take control again.

If you want an options robot, you need to know its strengths and weaknesses. Also, be aware that many false robots that are sold over the Internet, so the majority of those available are of no use to you. Many companies and brokers present the robots as being developed by experts, but you can never know who stands behind the invention and how good the so-called expert is. Therefore, thoroughly check all the aspects of the robot you would like to buy before you throw your money away on a useless tool.

The robot's benefits (only approved robots who do their job) are that they are able to make rational decisions, whereas you could potentially be overwhelmed by emotions that would cloud your thinking. They will also stick to the trading plan as set forth and not make irrational moves. They lack human emotions, so they will not be driven to make spontaneous decisions. Also, traders often make human errors, like changing their mind or simply clicking on something they shouldn't, whereby the robot cannot get tired, and it will not make mistakes.

The robots' main disadvantages would be that their decisions are based on previous analyses. So, if you place a trade and let the robot handle it, and a sudden market change happens that causes dramatic change, the robot will not be able to recognize it and will keep trading as planned. However, a trader would switch tactics in order to catch up with the new market developments. This clearly indicates that the human brain is still irreplaceable, and that the human hand is needed when it gets turbulent in the business.

CHAPTER 7: STRATEGIES AND TRADING PLANS

That we have discussed the options and tools that are at your disposal, let us take a look at the different strategies that can be applied when trading options. The tools can help you become a good trader, but the skills to implement them properly come from great trading strategies. Let us see what is important to create a trading strategy and which strategy is good in what situation.

Probably you have already noticed that a lot of factors are involved when it comes to the options industry, and maybe you are surprised by the range of knowledge you need if you want a successful trading career, but traders have to be aware that there is no such thing as easy or quick money. It has to be earned, one or way or another. Now, let us shift to the strategies that can be employed to optimize trading results.

Individual Trading

You can take a look at how other traders, especially the good ones, are handling their trades. It is certainly a good start to see how they interpret the market and how they make their trading decisions. This can help you a great deal with your trading decisions, but you cannot completely adopt someone else's way of trading. Each trading strategy is unique, and every trader views the market from their own perspective, so you will need to find a way to function in the market as someone who applies their own tricks and strategies. If you devote enough time to trading, you will develop your own trading style. It is like fashion; you have to do what seems right to you.

When you trade on your own, you automatically develop your trading skills, which means that in a few years you could have extraordinary skills and make a great deal of money with your knowledge. Training and development are crucial in every business, and binary options are not different.

Market Research

There is no way around studying and analyzing the market. You will always have to be in the loop with the latest market news if you want to understand the behavior of prices. Market analyses can be divided into technical analyses and fundamental analysis. Both have to be conducted from time to time. Your job is to read reports by financial analysts in order to get an idea of price movements.

Great indicators of market movements are economic news releases and international banks meetings. So, get familiar with the economic calendar and see when big news releases are scheduled each month, because that is a safe indicator that the market will fluctuate. News on inflation, PMI, GDP news, as well as retail stores news can all give you hints of how the market will behave.

For example, if it says that inflation is coming, you know that the prices will go up, which means that the market will be volatile for quite some time.

Chart Reading

After you have mastered the tools on the platforms, you need to understand how the charts work. The charts are inseparable from market analyses. They are basically the crystal ball that gives you hints of market behavior. The way trends move can tell you a lot about where the price is heading. First, you have to understand that there are different types of charts, like hourly charts, daily charts, and others. You can also use charts like candlestick charts, line charts, tick, and bar charts. All of them can help you make some profits.

The candlestick chart is named because it looks like a candle, and this chart contains more information than regular charts. It has a great visual display and makes it easier for traders to notice changes. The bar chart is somewhat easier and shows you the highest and the lowest course, as well as the opening and end course. Both of them are very convenient for short-term trades.

Once you learned to read the basics from a chart, you can move onto examining what shapes the trends take. When you gain enough experience, you will be able to identify triangles, waves, and ranges or channels, and what they represent. They usually indicate where the price is heading, giving you a clear advantage in the market. You will be able to predict price movements more accurately by following the different patterns. Still, to be able to do that, you will have to study the charts and the market a lot, by reading about the different movements and chart patterns.

Account Management and Robots

We have already talked about robots and their significance, so we will briefly reflect on that by stating that it is not bad to use robots from time to time, but it has to be under your supervision. You must be able to assess the situation properly to know when it is time to engage software assistance.

Account management is similar to using robots because it also means leaving trading decisions to someone else. If the broker offers you an account manager to help your trading, just make sure that it the manager is your friend. Managers sometimes work in favor of the broker and against you, and they can make poor trading decisions because they want the broker to win, not you. On the other hand, a decent account manager has more experience than you and will know how to get the best out of your trades. They will know where to invest your money and how to help you profit. Again, it requires a good manager who knows what he/she is doing to make money in the business.

Co-related Assets

Once you start to realize how the market works, you will figure out different ideas of how to trick the market (legally, of course), and one of the tricks can be trade-related assets. Usually, these assets are from the same industry and work on similar principles, which means that they are influenced by the same factors. They have similar, or the same, prices, and your job is to wait for a gap between the two.

This means that you are waiting for one of the assets to drop in value creating a gap. This gap represents the perfect opportunity to buy a put/call options, depending on the asset, before the assets even out in value. These gaps are usually short-term and can happen for different reasons, but the assets will eventually reach their pre-fluctuation state, and everything will go back to normal.

Be Smart and Cover Both Sides

Hedging and scalping are two well-known and well-loved strategies for traders. Hedging is a risk-reduction strategy, which works by buying and selling two different assets at the same time. It is a safety-net strategy, whereby traders can buy two correlated assets, but take opposite positions on each. For example, you can buy two different currency pairs, both of which involve the EUR. In one trade, you predict that the euro goes up, and in the other, that it will drop. Hedging is convenient for very risky trading circumstances, when a trader does not know how to assess the situation.

Also, you can buy an asset, and, at the same time, put it on sale with both trades running. Some brokers might forbid hedging, but it is widely accepted in Europe as a legal trading strategy. If you happen to lose in the first trade, you automatically win in your second, and that is the appeal. If your first asset recovers before expiry time and moves in your favor, you can quit or stop the second hedging position, and you will keep your money.

Hedging is not completely risk-free, and it can easily become riskier if someone does not know to hedge correctly. The prior market analysis is mandatory and you need a well-developed plan before engaging in hedging. Hedging has many sub-forms also, called indirect hedging, and they can turn be complicated. Unprepared traders often find themselves opening, closing, and reopening hedge positions, which can be very exhausting for the individual and their budget.

Scalping

Scalping is also a very common strategy, but it requires traders to trade for several hours a day, if they want a significant profit from the scalping strategy. This is especially suited for small-volume traders who make use of small daily gaps between the bid price and the ask price. The key is to get in and out of positions multiple times or buy at the bid price and sell at the ask price. The profits-per-trade are small, which means that a significant profit requires more trades.

The profits come from the bid-ask spread, and traders take the role of market makers here. The only important thing is that other traders are willing to buy the position offered. This strategy is only convenient for short-term trades and requires quick action. The ideal conditions for scalping are big market movements, so you might get on the market upon big news releases, when there is a lot of activity and buyers and sellers are all over the place.

Scalping is a very safe strategy, especially if compared to hedging, given that only small amounts are invested and gained. Buyers are not that hard to find, and there is always someone who will buy the option at the ask price. To be a scalper, one has to have the time and patience to possibly trade for a whole day or night. It requires focus, fast execution, and fast decision-making. Scalpers do not have the time to think through every decision, but they have to take their chance quickly and exercise a lot of self-discipline. Scalping is not the right strategy for big risk-takers or those who want the significant profit from a single trade.

As a beginner, scalping would be appropriate for you, even if it's just to see how it works and whether you have the discipline to carry out trade after trade. In the process, your investments will not suffer greatly. Scalping requires a trading platform that has direct buy and sell buttons because, with those, the trader will be able to react quickly.

Most trading platforms have these buttons, but check that option before you engage in scalping. The trades have to be planned carefully, because random trades will not create desirable results. You have to know what you are doing and which positions can be sold at the asking price. Again, market analysis represents the basis for successful scalping.

Combine All Strategies

You can also switch between these strategies and use a little bit of everything. The binary options market is not clear-cut, which means traders cannot use clear-cut options, because there are no rules that guarantee success. You have to be multi-faceted to employ different techniques and strategies every time you enter the market. Chart reading, market interpretation, good command of tools, and implementation of strategies are all important factors when building a trading career.

Planning and structuring are required if traders want to see their money double or triple. Information and data represent the core of all strategy building, and everything starts from there. You have to be willing to learn and apply the acquired knowledge in the industry, just like in any other job. The difference is that it is your money you invest, and you have to act in your own best interest.

Analyze the past movements of prices, and look at their behavior and what economic factors influence assets to rise or drop in value. That will give you a framework on which you can further build. You will be able to recognize similar behavioral patterns in real-time and in the future, which will enable you to make educated guesses and forecasts. Binary options is not a gambling game, but a well-defined business with a lot at stake, especially if you invest a great deal of money.

All of these strategies have brought in a great deal of money for traders, but they require a plan, patience, and knowledge. Study and train yourself to react appropriately when the opportunity is right. Sometimes you will need to scalp, and other times you will hedge or use robots.

CHAPTER 8: SUCCESSFUL TRADING

After we have discussed the different strategies and tools you can apply, let us discuss how to become a successful trader in the potentially lucrative, but hasty, market when competing with millions of other traders. The secret to success lies in your personal attitude towards trading, so you have to foster it in order to achieve the best results.

Do Not Get Disappointed Quickly

Many enter the market with a positive attitude, which is good, but after a series of losses, many will get discouraged and quit early. The binary options market is not a market where you can constantly win, and, in the beginning, you will probably experience lots of losses. Traders need to understand that not every trade is going to be successful, and they need to have a thick skin if they want to make it in the market. The main goal is for your winning trades to outnumber your losing trades, and that they prevail in general. No one ever wins every trade. In order to achieve the desired ratio, you will have to devote a lot of time into your trading career.

Take your Trades Seriously and Make a Plan

Binary options trading is not a random game, but requires a lot more effort than just sitting on your computer and clicking on random trades. First of all, make a trading plan. You can, for example, come up with a weekly schedule, displaying your trading time. Make room in your life for your trading career by devoting a couple of hours per day to trading. For example, you can trade every day from 6 pm to 8 or 9 pm, or if you are more a night person then from 10 pm until midnight. Everything is allowed, however, be sure not to deviate from your schedule since you need to come back regularly in order to make it pay off. Also, once you make a plan and decide how you are going to trade after you examined the market, stick to your given trading plan and do not let fear or panic change your decision, unless the market really turned upside down meanwhile.

Focus and Motivation

As previously said, options trading also needs your full attention. In a market that moves so quickly, you need to actively follow the course of your trades and even the slightest changes on the market. You have seen that chart reading can be sometimes complicated, so just make sure that you watch over the trends, prices, and their action. Try to stay away from social networks, your phone, or other distractions during your trading time. No one can be efficient in anything if they do not pay enough attention to it. Stay confident, even if things do not develop as planned. You cannot lose your spirit over small obstacles. Invest, plan, trade, and believe in yourself.

Invest Smart

As with your weekly time schedule, you also need to plan ahead for how much you are willing to invest. Put aside the amount of money that should cover your trades for a week. Then, divide that amount to cover your trades per day. This is a very important thing since many traders cannot stick to their investment plan and waste all their money on day one, especially when they are on a losing streak and try to invest further in order win back their money. Binary options trading does not work that way. It is not a Las Vegas casino, but a serious business. It is your business. You cannot keep investing until your trades look good because you will lose all your money, and you will cross the line from fine trading to gambling. Even if it is hard sometimes, and you end your trading session with a major loss, you need to know you can return the next day and work on earning that money back.

Multiple Brokers

You can join more than one broker, and you can use it to your advantage. Maybe one will have something the other lacks, like some special prices or bonuses. Do not restrict yourself to one kind of service when there are dozens of brokers who compete for dominance on the market. Their fight consists of offering different conveniences to traders, and you need every advantage you can get.

Emotions and Self-Discipline

Beginners tend to be overexcited when they enter the market and expect immediate results. Unfortunately, it will take some time until you will see real money in your account balance. Patience is key in this business and will get you far, if you are able to be disciplined. Trading can be a very emotional experience, especially because it concerns your hard-earned money, but you need to see it as a business that requires a cool head. You cannot base your decisions on emotions or gut feelings; you have to think like a businessman who needs to make something with their investment.

The broker is Not on Your Side

The simple truth is that the broker loses when you win, and that he wins when you lose. Brokers are market makers, and their business and success rely on traders' investments. Of course, they are not glad when they have to pay-out winnings since it means that they take money out of their own budget to pay the winners. Therefore, no matter how good and professional a broker is, they will not be happy when you win. When you trade, you trade against your broker; he is your only competition in the market during trades. You need to be aware that, sometimes, you will have to fight for your rights, especially since brokers sometimes tend to have a different point of view on the pay-out policy. This can even happen with the best broker, so you will need to know how your brokers work. For example, sometimes it can happen that the broker thinks that you did not meet all the requirements for a pay-out, but you know you did. This situation can be tricky and uncomfortable, but a trader who knows their rights will know how to handle their broker. Of course, you can always complain to the broker's licensor, but we would recommend such a step only in extreme situations.

CONCLUSION

The binary options market is and will always be turbulent, but I hope that beginners are now more prepared to cope in the market without being blindsided by the myths of the binary options world. The primary myth suggests that binary options produce easy money with little input, but this start-up guide shows that it indeed involves a lot of work to make it in the trading business. Beginners are now aware what awaits them when they join the risky market and how they can deal with it on an everyday basis. There will be sunny and rainy trading days, but traders will now know how to handle the pressure, how to approach their trades, and what it takes to make them profitable.

We have seen that many factors contribute to successful trading, like self-discipline, good trading skills, great command of the trading platform, and use of highly sophisticated tools and options. It is also important to do thorough market studies and analyses, to implement trading plans and strategies, and to properly allocate investments.

The guide explained how to find the right broker, how to know that he/she is a good broker, and how to determine whether a broker benefits you as a trader. The role of the broker is not to be neglected, given that the broker is your business partner and a lot of depends on their actions and professional behavior.

You also learned that the market is full of scammers who try to manipulate traders into investing, by pretending to be professional brokers. You also now know how to get around them. If you read this guide carefully, you will probably manage to avoid these false brokers because you will be able to recognize them. just like an experienced trader would.

The guide also emphasized the importance of charts and chart reading, whose importance many beginners tend to undermine. Now you know that the chart reveals half of the market secrets, and that the right interpretation of charts can lead you to desirable results.

Beginners now know that binary options has nothing to do with guessing, but with predicting the market on the basis of examinations, analyses, economic data, and economic news. They are aware that they have to dig deeply into the depths of the market to make the right trading decisions, which will bring them in considerable profits. Apart from their market knowledge, traders also know that their state of mind is an important contributor. They know that they should not give up when it gets tough, but should keep a good business head when a lot is at stake.

I sincerely hope that this start-up guide helped you understand what the binary options market is about and in what ways it can be profitable. The options market always involves a certain risk and nothing is certain until the very end, but that is what makes the market exciting, fun, and mysterious.

Thank you for taking the time to read this book. If you like this book, please leave us a review in Amazon. We would greatly appreciate your feedback.

www.ingramcontent.com/pod-product-compliance
Lightning Source LLC
Chambersburg PA
CBHW070715180526
45167CB00004B/1486